YOUR KNOWLEDGE HAS VALUE

AF153562

- We will publish your bachelor's and
  master's thesis, essays and papers

- Your own eBook and book -
  sold worldwide in all relevant shops

- Earn money with each sale

Upload your text at www.GRIN.com
and publish for free

Understanding the Fundamentals of Corporate Planning

Dr. David E. Amanawa

Bibliographic information published by the German National Library:

The German National Library lists this publication in the National Bibliography; detailed bibliographic data are available on the Internet at http://dnb.dnb.de.

ISBN: 9783389004487
This book is also available as an ebook.

Print and binding: Books on Demand GmbH, Norderstedt, Germany
Printed on acid-free paper from responsible sources.

The present work has been carefully prepared. Nevertheless, authors and publishers do not incur liability for the correctness of information, notes, links and advice as well as any printing errors.

GRIN web shop: https://www.grin.com/document/1448751

UNDERSTANDING THE FUNDAMENTALS OF CORPORATE PLANNING

By

Amanawa, David Ebiegberi (Ph.D.)

Faculty Member/Researcher at the Centre for Continuing Education, Ignatius Ajuru University of Education, Rivers State, Nigeria.

Abstract

In this article, Dr. Amanawa explains that corporate planning is a dynamic cycle that entails outlining a policy or procedure for an entire organization on a small, medium, or large scale. It means recognizing that the firm does not function in a vacuum and that its actions are influenced by what happens in its surroundings. Thus, this study's primary focus is to show management's capacity to comprehend the environment, make accurate forecasts, and then pick the best cause of action. Planning theory is a study of the nature and purpose of planning techniques; it may assist planners in comprehending their work's context, values, and repercussions and challenging and improving their practice. This discourse covers the topics of strategic planning, technological forecasting, socio-political forecasting, industry analysis, and operational planning.

Keywords: Corporate Planning, Strategic Planning, Forecasting, Industry Analysis

INTRODUCTION

Whether you are a startup aiming to land your first customer or an established corporation looking to reach a new market, corporate planning is essential to achieving your objectives.

Businesses utilize the corporate planning process to lay out a plan of action to expand, boost profitability, obtain visibility, or solidify brand identification. Successful companies use corporate planning to use their resources more effectively than their rivals.

According to Bochnewich (2015), it is critical to have a strategy in place regardless of the size of your company. A strategy may assist you not only in keeping your business organized but it can also help you increase the following:

- Clarity & Direction
- Ensure efficient use of resources
- Provide a way of measuring progress
- Support effective decision-making
- Coordinate activities
- Allocate responsibilities
- Motivate and guide staff

Elements of Planning

Before creating a business strategy, you must examine numerous variables as a company. You must step outside your company position and consider the following things as if you were a rival or a customer. You will need to do the following to establish an effective corporate plan:

- **Obtain Information:** Gathering information is the first and most crucial stage in developing a successful company plan. Consider the good, the terrible, the ugly, and the beautiful concerning your particular aims. You should obtain this data not just about your own business but also about your leading rivals. Regardless of how big or small your company is, it's critical to consider the advantages and disadvantages of the top players in your sector. This can help you form your strategy for avoiding other people's expensive blunders.
- **Set the Plan's Goals:** Although sometimes mistaken, the objectives and strategies are distinct. A broad principal result that may be quantified is a goal. The method you use to accomplish that aim is called a strategy.
- **Create Tactics to Achieve Your Objectives:** The word S.M.A.R.T. stands for Specific, measurable, Attainable, Relevant, and Time-bound; these five criteria can assist you in creating realistic objectives, completing them in a fair amount of time and evaluating the outcomes. The acronym was created by George Doran, Arthur Miller, and James Cunningham and published in 1981 in an essay titled "There's a S.M.A.R.T. Way to Write Management's Goals and Objectives" (Jakubic et al. 2016).
- **Put your Strategy into Action:** Implementation planning is a project management technique that provides step-by-step instructions for project completion. This procedure informs project team members of the activities and individual duties needed to fulfill the team's strategic goals. When you implement anything, such as a plan, you guarantee that what was intended is completed.
- **Keep an Eye on the Plan's Performance:** A performance plan is a document that assists in tracking and assessing the outcomes of interventions during a program. It is an ever-changing document that should be referred to and updated frequently. While the specifics of each program's plan will vary, they should all adhere to the same fundamental framework and include the same critical aspects.
- **Assess the Effectiveness/Success of your Strategy:** To assess the success and efficiency of an organization's strategy, consider how it connects your goals to how you want to attain them and the methods you intend to employ. A strategy is effective if it employs the resources you want to devote and produces the desired results.

By creating a business plan, you will feel secure in every decision you make. You will have a road plan that you can confidently follow since you have done your homework and calculated the statistics. If you're having trouble articulating the legal ramifications of your strategy, an estate planning attorney can help. Failure to plan can soon lead to failure to plan.

The study of the concepts, principles, and assumptions that underpin planning as a social activity is known as planning theory. It investigates planning's aims, functions, procedures, and ethical, political, and epistemological difficulties. Planning theory is a complex and dynamic discipline representing several viewpoints, ideologies, and traditions rather than a single, cohesive body of knowledge.

Planning theory is critical because it may help planners understand and guide their decisions and actions in complicated and dynamic circumstances. Planning theory may also assist planners in critically reflecting on their beliefs, attitudes, and prejudices and how these impact their job. Furthermore, planning theory may assist planners in communicating and justifying their ideas and plans and engaging with other stakeholders and disciplines.

Evaluating planning theory is a complicated and subjective endeavor since various theories have different criteria, norms, and goals. The relevance and usefulness of planning practice and policy, its coherence and consistency with other theories and evidence, its ethical and democratic values and implications, and its innovation and creativity in terms of concepts and methods are possible ways to assess planning theory.

Comparing planning theories is challenging and subjective since various theories have different assumptions, scopes, and emphases. To compare planning theories, one must analyze their ontological, epistemological, and normative underpinnings and their aims, roles, and planning procedures. Furthermore, one must analyze each theory's findings, suggestions, and consequences, as well as their views, paradigms, and traditions. These variables can influence how compatible, complementary, contradictory, inclusive, or exclusive each theory is.

STRATEGIC PLANNING

Strategic planning is developing precise business plans, implementing them, and analyzing the results concerning a company's long-term goals or wants. It is a concept that focuses on integrating multiple departments inside a firm (such as accounting and finance, marketing, and human resources) to achieve strategic goals. Strategic planning and strategic management are essentially interchangeable terms.

Strategic planning first gained popularity in the 1950s and 1960s, and it remained popular in the corporate world until the 1980s when it fell out of favor; however, enthusiasm for strategic business planning was reignited in the 1990s, and strategic planning remains relevant in modern business.

Strategic Planning Process

Upper-level management must devote critical thinking and preparation to the strategic planning process. Executives may explore various possibilities before deciding on a course of action and how to implement it strategically. Finally, a company's management will, hopefully, agree on a strategy that is most likely to produce positive results (usually defined as increasing the company's bottom line) and that can be executed cost-effectively with a high likelihood of success while avoiding undue financial risk.

Strategic planning development and execution are commonly considered as being accomplished in three critical steps:

- **Strategy Formulation:** A corporation will conduct an internal and external audit to evaluate its current status before developing a plan. This is done as part of a SWOT analysis to assist in determining the organization's strengths and weaknesses as well as opportunities and threats. The study helps managers determine which strategies or markets to pursue or forgo, how to use the company's resources effectively, and whether to expand operations through a merger or joint venture. Business strategies have a long-term impact on the performance of organizations. The authority to allocate the resources required for its implementation typically only extends to high management leaders.

- **Strategy Implementation:** The organization must commit resources for its execution after formulating a plan of action and setting precise targets or goals for its implementation. How well senior management communicates the selected strategy across the organization and persuades everyone to "buy into" the desire to implement the plan can frequently influence how well the implementation stage goes. Creating a solid foundation for the strategy's execution, making the most of available resources, and refocusing marketing activities to align with the strategy's goals and objectives are all necessary for effective strategy implementation.

- **Strategy Evaluation:** Any astute businessman knows that today's success does not guarantee future success. As a result, managers must assess the effectiveness of a chosen strategy following the implementation stage. Reviewing the internal and external elements impacting the strategy's execution, monitoring performance, and taking corrective action to improve the plan's effectiveness are the three critical components of strategy evaluation. For instance, a business could learn that to achieve the required changes in customer relations, it has to acquire a new customer relationship management (CRM) software package after adopting a plan to enhance customer service.

All three stages of strategic planning take place in the three hierarchical levels of high management, middle management, and operational levels. It is crucial to encourage communication and interaction among employees and managers at all levels to enable the company to work as a more functional and successful team.

Benefits of Strategic Planning

Due to the unstable business climate, many businesses use reactive rather than proactive methods. Reactive methods may need a significant investment of time and money to implement, yet they are often only effective in the short term. Strategic planning enables businesses to take a more long-term approach to problem-solving and proactive planning. They allow a business to exert influence rather than merely react to circumstances.

According to CFI (2020), the following are some of the main advantages of strategic planning:

Table 1. Benefits of Strategic Planning

BENEFITS	FUNCTIONS
Helps formulate better strategies using a logical, systematic approach	This is probably the most significant advantage. Regardless of the effectiveness of a particular strategy, several studies indicate that the strategic planning process itself significantly contributes to enhancing a company's overall performance.
Enhanced communication between employers and employees	The effectiveness of the strategic planning process depends on communication. It is started via involvement and communication between management and staff, demonstrating their dedication to accomplishing corporate goals.

	Managers and staff may demonstrate their dedication to the organization's aims with the aid of strategic planning. This is so because they know the business's operations and motivations. When organizational goals and objectives are made concrete via strategic planning, employees can better appreciate the connection between their performance, the success of the business, and remuneration. Consequently, both staff members and management have a greater capacity for innovation and creativity, which promotes the company's further expansion.
Empowers individuals working in the organization	Employees' perceptions of their contribution to the success of the organization as a whole are strengthened by enhanced discussion and communication throughout the whole process. Due to this, businesses must decentralize the strategic planning process by including employees and lower-level managers across the whole organization. An excellent example is the Walt Disney Company, which abolished its strategic planning section to distribute the planning responsibilities across the many Disney business divisions.

Source: Compiled by Author

Strategic planning is being used by more and more businesses to create and carry out sound choices. Even though it takes a lot of time, money, and effort to plan, a well-thought-out strategic plan effectively promotes business development, goal attainment, and employee happiness.

TECHNOLOGICAL FORECASTING

Technology has largely influenced how human beings have changed throughout the years. Managers in both public and commercial enterprises have lately come to understand the need to anticipate technology development and how it may affect their operations. Forecasts for the economy, the stock market, the financial system, and the weather are now standard management tools. Technology forecasting, which is still in its infancy, must soon catch up to these other analytical tools regarding acceptance and usefulness.

Technological Forecasting (TF) studies emerging trends, novel technologies, and forces that may result from the interaction of several elements, such as evolving societal concerns, governmental initiatives, and scientific advancements. These forces are outside specific companies' knowledge, influence, and control.

People in business contemplate things like the following when they consider the advantages of technological forecasting in their organizations (Quinn, 1967):

- What objectives does technology forecasting serve?
- What types of techniques and strategies are working well?
- What are the strengths and weaknesses of these strategies?
- How should businesses set themselves up for technological forecasting?
- What additional information and methods are required to increase the usefulness of forecasts?

Purpose of Technological Forecasting

First, let us clarify a significant cause of misunderstanding in technological forecasting: the objective of this activity. To be practical, technological projections do not have to anticipate the exact shape technology will take in a particular application at some future date. Their objective, like any other projection, is to assist managers in evaluating the likelihood and significance of various potential future occurrences so that they may make better decisions.

What Technology Can Be Predicted

However, how can a technological prediction be created to include probability dimensions in the same way that other predictions do? Most people associate "technology" with a very particular physical object. They don't consider this as possessing the changeable qualities that allow for probability or range projections. They believe that a properly defined technology will either exist in a specific circumstance or not. Furthermore, the forecaster must accurately foresee this occurrence, or else he is mistaken. Much of the misunderstanding in talks about technical forecasting stems from this erroneous belief, which would put an untenable burden on any forecaster.

The truth is that a "technology" is not just one unchangeable component of chemistry or hardware. Simply put, it is the systematic application of knowledge—knowledge of physical relationships—to the useful arts. Over time, this information may change continually. It can range from the first inklings of how fundamental phenomena can be used to address a real-world issue to a finished object, equipment, or industrial tool in an established operating system.

Even in this situation, any equipment, product, or operating system typically experiences gradual, incremental improvements over time. What could seem to be a "step function" progress in technology is typically nothing more than a collection of little improvements that are not worth adopting until they sum up to a significant shift in the technology as a whole. Additionally, a particular technology typically has a wide range of competing products, each with a unique combination of performance and affordability that only appeals to specific demographics. Finally, a particular technological process or product may also satisfy different demands and carry out very different roles for its numerous owners.

Technology forecasting is made feasible by the relative consistency of a technology's technical, economic, and prospective applications. It is pointless for the forecaster to attempt to foretell the precise kind and form of the technology that will dominate a given future application unless they make immediate direct extrapolations of existing approaches. However, he can predict the performance qualities that a specific usage will likely require by making "range forecasts." He can predict the performance qualities that a specific class of technology will be able to offer by specific future dates. Additionally, by the anticipated dates, he can consider the possible effects of possessing these technological and economic capabilities.

Value of Technology Forecasting for Management

It is possible to compare technology projections to market or economic forecasts in several ways. Any savvy manager would not count on market projections to accurately estimate market size or features. He would be aware that there is almost no chance of accurately estimating the precise monetary amount of a future market. However, he may legitimately request that his market analysts calculate a market's most probable or "expected" size and assess the likelihoods and effects of various sizes. Similarly, intelligent people can often make meaningful predictions about "expected" future technology capabilities and assess the likelihood and ramifications of variances from them. As an example, consider the following forecast:

Surprisingly, some people advocate against using technical predictions in executive decision-making. They stress that predicting technology developments is still an art. These skeptics contest the value of predicting since two or more independent specialists viewing the same phenomenon might reach wildly divergent judgments. A lack of faith in the potential management applications for the projections exacerbates their worries about accuracy. They worry that the forecaster's ego may cause him to exaggerate his predictions. They also fear that managers would accept projections without hesitation and without understanding their limitations.

Such viewpoints lack perspective and are incredibly damaging; because of this, economists, financial analysts, and market forecasters can view the same data and reach different conclusions about the future. Additionally, their predictions may be overstated or misapplied. Would those who object to technical forecasting also dispute the value of such initiatives? How can they account for the reality that managements already use technology predictions daily?

By defining future technology possibilities and risks more precisely, technological projections can help decision-makers make better choices. Forecasts do not always need to give accurate knowledge about the future to enhance judgments. Complete accuracy is not a reasonable expectation, nor is it required to justify predicting expenses. Forecasts must enable a better operation than would be possible without them to be valuable. And they need to contribute more to decisions than what it costs to prepare them.

One wonders how their management can afford to ignore these issues since technology uncertainty is among many businesses' most significant challenges. For executives who make policy, well-made technology projections—the type of forecasts that account for technological uncertainties—should easily justify their costs. And as they do now with marketing or financial projections, wise managers must also learn to use these forecasts. Their other option is to keep their heads in the sand and make decisions based only on educated guesses about emerging technology. It is reckless to act in this way.

Socio-Political Forecasting

Socio-political systems and problems involve a combination of social and political factors. It is possible to predict sales with some accuracy mathematically. Realistically, though, external economic and market circumstances beyond your control might diminish this accuracy. Some of the outside elements that may have an impact on sales include the following:

- **Political Stability:** Political unrest in a particular region may impact government policy announcements, impacting an organization's sales prediction for a specific period. Consider analyzing potential animosity between a company's home country and the nation hosting its international market. The study is done to forecast how a break in diplomatic ties (and potential economic retaliation) could affect the company's sales from international markets.

- **Population Trends:** Sales generally are directly impacted by the overall economic activity. Sales are anticipated to rise during economic booms and to fall during downturns, all other things being equal. If the sales manager is to be a capable sales forecaster, they must be an efficient forecaster of future company circumstances. He must thus be knowledgeable about numerous economic activity indicators and thoroughly understand how the economy functions. He has to be current on the state of the economy.
- **Style and Fashion:** In several industries, fashion is gaining importance. Forecasting sales are more challenging when a business sells items dependent on trends and fads. This is because everything depends on how well the market receives the fashions the company intends to sell. Modifications in fashion and style can have a good or negative impact on sales volume. If not adequately predicted, this might render a forecaster's job meaningless. Nobody, however, can foresee such shifts with any degree of precision. Styles and trends are therefore seen to increase risk in predicting.
- **Price Levels:** The state of the industry will affect a company's sales volume. As a result, changes in the direct and indirect competitive market circumstances will impact the company's future sales volume. The number of rivals may vary, or their marketing strategies may alter, including product design, advertising, promotional campaigns, etc. For instance, the entry of Globacom into the Nigerian GSM market changed the industry's pricing structure (to pay by the second pricing plan). It affected it because MTN dominated the industry before its entry, and call rates were charged by the minute.
- **Consumer Earnings:** The quantity of consumer income in the economy will inevitably impact consumers' disposable income and, consequently, their purchasing power. A sales forecaster must know consumer earnings in the market under consideration.
- **Weather:** Sales volume is influenced by weather and fluctuations in it. Due to the demand for consumers to "cool down," businesses that deal in soft drinks, bottled water, and brewers see brisk sales during the hot season. While some retailers report sales decline on rainy days or weeks, other businesses selling umbrellas, cardigans, sweaters, and other wet weather essentials report sales volume increases.

From the aforementioned sociopolitical difficulties, it can be inferred that some of the above-mentioned external elements may significantly impact the accuracy of any company's forecasting. If these aspects are not considered, the results of any forecasting processes will be worthless.

In conclusion, the results of business forecasting may not be entirely correct owing to some of the variables mentioned above, such as the inaccuracy of the internal data that is currently accessible, the laboriousness of the approach used, and occasionally the expense of forecasting. Additionally, there may be variables that forecasters cannot control, such as the price level and rate of inflation, the degree of political and economic stability, etc.

INDUSTRY ANALYSIS

Businesses employ various methods to comprehend their market and keep a competitive edge. Analyzing specific characteristics of an industry is a crucial step in understanding market dynamics in a given sector. Understanding their rivals, using their strengths, minimizing risks, and providing clients with better service may all be facilitated by learning how to do this study (Indeed, 2022).

Businesses and analysts use industry analysis as a technique for market analysis to comprehend an industry's competitive dynamics. It aids in their understanding of the state of an industry, including statistics on demand and supply, level of industry competition, industry's competitiveness with other emerging industries, industry's prospects in light of technological advancements, its credit system, and the impact of outside factors (CFI, 2020).

An organization may detect prospective risks and opportunities, anticipate future market changes, and make strategic plans to maintain its market position with the insights from this study. These assessments can assist investors in determining if an investment in a company will be lucrative in the long run, in addition to providing enterprises with a comprehensive understanding of their operational environment.

In a research carried out by the Small Business Accelerator Program of the University of British Columbia in 2012, a checklist was proposed and is shown in the table below:

Table 2. Checklist for Industry Analysis

CHECKLIST	FUNCTION
Identify your industry and provide a brief overview.	It would help if you researched your sector on a local, regional, provincial, national, and international level. Make careful to specify any applicable industry codes. Depending on current and past economic conditions, provide statistics and historical data regarding the nature of the industry and the development potential for your company.
Summarize the nature of the industry.	Include precise details like growth trends, economic volatility, and projected income. Keep up with the latest advancements, news, and developments. Discuss marketing tactics and the prevailing operational and managerial trends in the sector.
Provide a forecast for your industry.	Assemble industry forecasts and economic data across several time horizons (5, 10, and 20 years). Cite your sources accurately. Please note that the information you may get on a particular industry will depend on its size and kind. Indicate whether it is new, developing, increasing, mature, or diminishing.
Identify government regulations that affect the industry.	Include any recently passed legislation affecting your sector and any licenses or permits required to operate in your target market. This section may provide information about fees and associated expenses.
Explain your unique position within the industry.	List the top firms in the sector and produce a summary of the information about your direct and indirect competitors after your competitive analysis is complete. This will assist you in articulating your distinctive value proposition.
List potential limitations and risks.	Write about potential disadvantages to your firm and your predictions for the near and far future. List the driving factors you know, including new laws, technology, globalization, rivalry, and shifting consumer demands.

Talk to people	Visit trade exhibits, make telephone calls, chit-chat with members of relevant associations, and attend business gatherings.

Source: (UBC, 2021)

Other industry analysis tools include:

SWOT Analysis

The SWOT analysis analyses the opportunities, threats, weaknesses, and strengths that might affect an organization. Managers concentrate on two elements when doing this analysis:

- **Internal Factors:** The study evaluates a company's internal strengths and weaknesses, which are the elements that might impact how well it operates and competes in a market. Talent, unique technology, a more significant market share, or a profitable product or service can all be considered strengths. The study pinpoints tactics for minimizing flaws and capitalizing on strengths for increased business effectiveness and performance.
- **External Factors:** Opportunities and weaknesses are considered in a SWOT analysis. Competitors with more advanced technology or effective marketing and sales departments might be weak. It assesses how risks to the sector can affect the organization and look for solutions to lessen their detrimental consequences. The study evaluates the company's possibilities to strengthen its competitive advantage.

PESTLE Analysis

The political, economic, social, technical, legal, and environmental (PESTLE) aspects that might impact a firm are assessed. Following are some analysis-related considerations.

- **Politics:** Government policies, trade restrictions, tariffs, and the general political atmosphere of the region where a firm operates or plans to operate are all evaluated as part of the analysis.
- **Economy:** In this study area, variables including Gross Domestic Product (GDP), net income, imports and exports, unemployment rate, interest rates, availability to credit, and taxation are examined.
- **Social Issues:** The analysis assesses social elements such as the local populace's demography, client purchasing patterns, and sentiments.
- **Technology:** The analysis also assesses how a firm may be impacted by technology, including Internet usage, market trends, and research and development initiatives.
- **Legal Aspects:** This examines how other legal obligations, such as industry rules, employee contracts, and labor legislation, may affect a firm.
- **Environment:** In this analysis, the future effects of environmental problems, including climate change, on the company are examined.

Michael Porter's Five Forces

Managers use Michael Porter's Five Forces to study an industry efficiently by evaluating five factors.

- **Rivalry with Competitors:** To comprehend that industry, a company must understand its position concerning rivals in the same industry. The number of businesses offering the same good or service and the market share of each rival determine the amount of competition a firm must contend with. The number of goods each business sells, operating costs, and governmental laws may all impact the competition. If several businesses in a given sector provide the same goods, the level of competition will continue to be fierce.
- **The Threat of Potential Entrants:** Existing businesses are likely to endure less rivalry and experience more extended periods of profitability if it is harder for new businesses to enter the sector. Reduced entry barriers, on the other hand, can portend future increased competition and reduced profits as rivals fight for market share.
- **The Threat of Substitutes:** Products or services that fulfill the same purpose are substitutes. Because consumers will move to an alternative when a product's price rises, a sector where businesses supply alternatives will likely see intense competition. The possibility of replacement enhances competition and might force businesses to invest more in differentiating their goods from rivals to keep customers from purchasing alternatives.
- **Buyers' Bargaining Power:** Customers' negotiating ability can also alter how fiercely a market is competitive. The buyers have less negotiating leverage in a market when there are few providers and many consumers. Cheaper buyer negotiating power prevents customers from pressuring vendors to offer premium goods and services at cheaper costs, which can boost vendors' profitability. When there are more suppliers than demand, buyers have more negotiating power, negatively impacting profitability.
- **Sellers Bargaining Power:** The number of suppliers in a particular sector of the economy may give such suppliers sway over enterprises. The suppliers may boost prices if a company has a limited number of suppliers for the raw materials needed to make its best-selling product. Increased pricing may result in higher manufacturing expenses since the company has limited other options for obtaining its raw materials. The company may absorb the additional expenses and lose money, or it can pass them on to consumers and run the risk of them switching to alternatives. Businesses often have more negotiating leverage in sectors with more suppliers because they have more options for obtaining their raw materials.

As a method of market evaluation, industry analysis is essential since it aids in a company's understanding of market dynamics. It aids in forecasting supply and demand and the firm's financial results. It shows the level of industry competition and the expenses of joining and leaving the market. It is crucial while preparing for a small business. An industry's present stage may be determined by analysis, including whether it is still expanding, has room for growth, or has reached its saturation point.

Entrepreneurs can grasp the industry's processes and find untapped prospects by thoroughly researching the sector. It's also critical to know that industry analysis is not always accurate and does not ensure success. Entrepreneurs may make poor judgments or follow the wrong route if data is misinterpreted. It is crucial to gather data as a result properly.

OPERATIONAL PLANNING

Based on a strategic plan, operational planning develops a comprehensive roadmap. The operational plan coordinates the dates, action items, and significant milestones that finance or the business must meet to carry out the strategic plan. In this sense, an operational plan explains the organization's primary objectives and goals and clarifies how it will achieve them.

The outcome of a team or department working to carry out a strategic plan is operational planning. To ensure the success of team-based activities that support the strategic plan, it is a process that looks to the future and maps out department goals, capabilities, and budgets.

Operational business plans work best when all members of the team or department are on board since this increases the likelihood that problems will be brought to light, goals will be established, deadlines will be met, and business collaboration will be more successful. Operational plans function much more effectively to guarantee that the entire organization meets its objectives when there is communication between finance and the business.

Critical Steps of Operational Planning

A well-thought-out company operational plan ensures that team members collaborate seamlessly, that everyone understands what has to be done and their role, and that crucial choices concerning long-term strategy are guided. According to (Planful, 2022), the following steps should be followed:

- Define the goal or vision for the operational plan clearly.
- Analyze and identify critical business stakeholders, resources, and budget team members, budgets, and resources.
- Consistently track and inform team members and stakeholders on progress.
- Adapt the operational plan to broaden company goals as needed.

Various factors influence who develops operational plans:

- **Scope:** The operational strategy for each action contains the who, what, and when and must be laser-focused on the initiative and the team. Make sure the scope isn't overly vast.
- **Timeline:** Depending on the organization's pace and velocity, an operational plan should include a quarter, six months, or a fiscal year.
- **Stakeholders:** To correctly estimate what work should be included in the plan, operational planning stakeholders should be close to the task. From tactical details to strategic execution, finance must unite the enterprise.

The operational plan is often the domain of middle management, in contrast to the strategic plan, which receives top-down implementation from the C-suite. Its scope is likewise narrowing as everyday activities are planned and constantly evolving. Strategic plan changes will be less frequent. Middle managers are frequently best suited to map out and implement the operational strategy because they focus on day-to-day operations, resource allocation, and duties.

CONCLUSION

According to Vaidya (2023), corporate planning is the process of establishing long-term objectives and goals within the framework of an organization to create an environment favorable to revenue and profit margin expansion. It includes developing plans, making decisions, and allocating resources. The corporate planning strategy assists the whole team in working in unison toward the organization's goals. Furthermore, a corporate planning cycle is a dynamic and ongoing activity that occurs throughout the life of an organization. Corporate planning identifies obstacles that may impede progress towards predetermined goals, and management can give ways to overcome them. Furthermore, it enables the organization to manage its resources better.

Fig. 1. Life Cycle of Corporate Planning

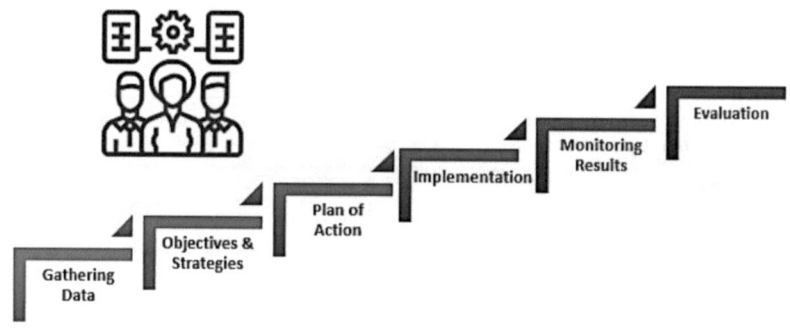

Extensive preparation for the future enables firms to better deal with various problems. Running a business is fraught with uncertainty and hazards. On the other hand, an effective corporate strategy assists the organization by anticipating risk value in the future, decreasing the risk of ambiguity.

A well-defined strategy assists staff in better understanding their duties. Furthermore, because all workers understand their jobs, the organization has less friction and greater togetherness. A better success rate may be predicted with employee participation and continuous development of procedures within the organization's scope, objectives, and strategies, which are easier to implement.

References

Bochnewich. (2015). *6 Elements of Successful Corporate Planning*. Retrieved from B-Trust Law: https://www.btrustlaw.com/blog/6-elements-of-successful-corporate-planning/#:~:text=Corporate%20planning%20is%20a%20process,more%20wisely%20th an%20their%20competitors.

CFI. (2020). *Industry Analysis: Understanding the competitiveness of an industry*. Retrieved from CFI Education Inc.: https://corporatefinanceinstitute.com/resources/management/industry-analysis-methods/

CFI. (2020). *Strategic Planning*. Retrieved from CFI Education Inc.: https://corporatefinanceinstitute.com/resources/management/strategic-planning/

Indeed. (2022). *Industry Analysis: Definition, Types, Aspects and Steps*. Retrieved from Ocean Financial Centre: https://sg.indeed.com/career-advice/career-development/industry-analysis

Jakubik, L., Eliades, A., Weese, M., & Huth, J. (2016). Mentoring Practice and Mentoring Benefit 2: Mapping the Future and Career Optimism - An Overview and Application to Practice Using Mentoring Activities. Pediatric Nursing, 42(3), 145.

Planful. (2022). *Operational Planning*. Retrieved from The Financial Performance Platform: https://planful.com/operational-planning/#:~:text=Operational%20planning%20is%20the%20result,to%20support%20the%20strategic%20plan.

Quinn, J. (1967). Technological Forecasting. *Harvard Business Review*.

UBC. (2021). *Industry Analysis*. Retrieved from Small Business Accelerator Program: https://sba.ubc.ca/business-basics/beginners-guide-business-research/industry-analysis

Vaidya, D. (2023). *Corporate Planning*. Retrieved from Wallstreet Mojo: https://www.wallstreetmojo.com/corporate-planning/#:~:text=Corporate%20planning%20is%20setting%20long,%2Dmaking%2C%20and%20allocating%20resources.

YOUR KNOWLEDGE HAS VALUE

- We will publish your bachelor's and
  master's thesis, essays and papers

- Your own eBook and book -
  sold worldwide in all relevant shops

- Earn money with each sale

Upload your text at www.GRIN.com
and publish for free